after
apocalypse

365 days
8760 hours
525600 minutes
31536000 seconds

to grow
into someone i'd call my
forever home

t w e n t y t w e n t y o n e

don't you get too close
to a poet
and don't hurt them
they'll turn you into mighty words
that will shiver down your
spine
and everyone who knows them
will know your name
without them every mentioning a
single syllable

dianne madison foit 2021

for lea

who inspired me to start writing again

for teresa

who is my safe place after all

and for felix

who never stopped believing in me

"This is the voice in your head that says, "You do not want this"

This is the ache that says, "You do not want him"

This is the glimmer of light that you're keepin' alive

When you tell yourself, "Bet I could fuck him"

Why do you need love so badly?

Bet it's because of her daddy

Bet she was brutal and bratty

Bet that she'll never be happy"

Halsey, "Whispers"

- *or a song that i would have needed many many months ago*

chapter one

winter

and the first tragedy

it's even more horrendous
when you clearly
know

you tried everything you
could
he tried everything he
could

and both of us remain toxic and
disappointed

the forever that i wanted to mean
was
n e v e r

meant
to
be

-tragedy nr.1

i was never a lesbian
i was suffering from
internalized
biphobia

while having casual sex
which i hate

but the more i don't wanna be something
the more i pretend that i am
something else

and i'm wandering from
attachment to
attachment
to falling for someone
new again

they seem so
perfect in my idealizing
brain

you got me heavily

you're not a man you are better than
them
my queen of
darkness

i'm crying in my sheets
with this new
girl

i'm crying in the sheets
of some stranger
like 10 years older than
me

all i want is to be
sexual
again

but it's so hard to
find yourself again like
that

when you've been ruined
again

even though he promised to be
different

i was addicted to my
mom
but i'm letting go
but projected the fears she left
in me

onto my bestie
who became my safe place after
i left and was
left behind

-it explains so much, it scares me

the lack of someone
sexually being
attracted to me and
showing it

made me sell my body
sell my
soul

to receive less than planned
and being disgusted afterwards

-prostitution, one time, never again

when i kinda tried to
admit my feelings
showing you the song

"flawless"
with the quote

"i just can't wait for love to destroy us"

i wasn't expecting it to actually happen

like, now i know i destroyed you
too

but i know i was hurting to
traumatic points

you might deserve an apology from
me but i deserve an apology from

the world
who made me like that

who made me think i had to
stay

who didn't give me other options

mono-amatonormativity is
traumatic

-tragedy nr.1

i cried in stranger's arms
while senselessly fucking
everyone who seemed
nice
to break my own heart

with you again,
it seemed so perfect

and i cried over
it

not about your love
not about our future

you made me see **no**
future
after all

i am my own future

i can't go back to
normal
after splitting
after trauma
after torture

it's not your fault,
it's mine.
it's not my fault,
it's yours.

it's about all and none of
us.

just a disaster that taught me a lot
about myself
but don't you DARE expect me
to still be your friend now.

-tragedy nr. 1

would have been our
anniversary
tomorrow
two years we said
forever

i meant it
bpd obsession
meant it
my aromantic ass
didn't
the heavy splitting
didn't

my **loyalty** *did.*

we've been a group of three

you two have each other
i have no one
left

no one that i don't need though

polyamory shows me

that my kind of love
is just as valid as
any other kind
that my view on love
is realistic
and that being vulnerable
and intimate
is nothing to only share
with one person

and most importantly

that i am complete
on my own

mbti
is more than just a
test

it's about understanding
oneself
one's surroundings
connecting

and understanding why some
connections
appear much harder
than others.

it's saving me

-i have no clue how it started tho

i thought 2021
would be the end for
me nothing to
be glad about
look forward to
enjoy

you leaving five days in
made me realize
you were the heaviness
not the
happiness
that i considered you to
be
-tragedy nr. 1

and i kissed a few more
mouths
some new some old
some wrong some
right
touched some people closer

more than the years before

feeling free

desired and

accepted

by others but finally by
myself
-after tragedy nr.1

i sold you my whole
body

and you didn't hesitate
to use me

of course, you didn't have
fun i couldn't fake my
interest

not at all

but promising 200 and giving me
50

is just fucking disgusting

i'm the one who
misses
i'm the one who
aches
i'm the one who has a hundred
friends

but no one shows me love
in the way i
need it

maybe it's not true
but the way i over-love

everyone

is just way too fucking much

if i ever felt any
intense
emotions about you

be sure

i will never get over you
and even ten years later

the thought of you
takes my breath

and sleep at
night

-bpd love

of course,
they won't understand
if i don't explain

but if i try to
explain
they might refuse to understand

it's hard enough for them to
get stuff about
depression
anxiety

so now dissociation
specific eating disorders
or misophonia

nobody gives a shit
and i end up suffering
alone

my phone makes me feel
safe
if i don't take it
everywhere

anxiety will eat me
alive

-bet you won't understand but still

autumn of 2020, the beginning
of winter
when i listened to
walking on cars
trying to convince
myself

i was happy

but let's face it
being with you made me
lose myself

made me stay stuck

and when you set me
free

i blossomed
and somehow i hope, you do
too

but honestly
i don't believe in it

because if i learned one thing
if you don't want
help
you won't get better

-tragedy nr.1

having an
instagram community
that feels more like family
than the blood one
does

you are lucky and fucked up
at the same
time

having bpd means
you'll get your heart broken
not just over people
over every single thing
that happens
'cause

we
feel
too
m u c h

chapter two
spring
and the second tragedy

when you said you don't get
the whole
marriage
romance?

whatever

thing

i was devastated because

i was addicted to and obsessed with
you

little did i know

we have more in common than i
thought

-my possibly aroace infp ex, tragedy nr.1

i might feel like i

failed but

compare it to
the years before

we'd rather name it the

opposite

water
my biggest fear

it keeps alive

and kills
if you use it wrong

just like an fp

that's why both appear so

scary to me

when i was twelve
and depression started to
cover me and everything
i ever had
i cried
thinking i'd open my eyes at eighteen
being perfectly fine

for once
again

little me, you were so wrong
but you're alive
and started living

you didn't think you'd make it to
eighteen

next year you'll be twenty

studying german studies
the stuff you loved in tenth grade
living in your own apartment
being a singer and a pole dancer
taking your hands to write
again

because so much happened in a
year

from twelve to twenty
you should know
you're the biggest survivor of your time

i tried to be with people

when i didn't love myself
i craved someone to hold me
because i couldn't do it
for myself
but as i'm healing
i never wanted it
it's not what i aim for
i know better now

but i'm forever thankful for the experience

walking down the hills
wuppertal and certain streets
neuss and empty parking lots
hot showers
listening to this one song and feeling and feeling and
feeling

nothing.
not at all.

don't tell me i
didn't try

-self-forced romance, part x

"she was beautiful, but she didn't mean a thing to me"

i wish i didn't relate to this
line
and had to think of her
immediately

while all i wanted was to be
in love
with her as well

-tragedy nr. 2

you're not worth more
because you weigh
less

-something my mom refuses to understand

with wet eyes
an increasing heartbeat
forcing everything trying the best i
could

stuttering
whining

"my brain tells me that i can't love you"

i said, overwhelmed

on our tenth month-versary
when i made you breakfast on the
balcony

trying my hardest to feel at least
something

of course, you were hurt
but

you know,
your lack of sexuality exactly did the same
to me

and it's not like i just can't love
you

i'm
aromantic

i don't love anyone that way
and this is okay

we didn't know any better
in 2019
anyway

-tragedy nr.1

and they'll be sleeping through the
days
staying up through half the
nights

every single kid in town found their own reason to
survive

sometimes
i just wanna be
like you

the perspective
turn it
around

i don't wanna be broken
i'm not
just wish i had known earlier

-allosexual aromantic

people just don't ger it
social distancing
brought me to
my
knees

if i did it more
i probably would have taken

my
own
life

y'all can listen
save everyone

i needed to save myself first

i thought it was quite
normal
to get into relationships without
feelings

trying to convince myself i felt
it
finally and hard enough

only for attention

i don't give a damn

so sorry to my exes
i might have been obsessed with
some of you

but true love won't arise from
me

not in romantic nature

with two personality disorders
you can't do anything
right

it's clearly impossible

you promise yourself that
you will finally know how to
be better

but end up to be
hurtful again

in the end

why can't i just act right for
once

please?....

i hate pretending
so much
and i continue it

so many people are bad for
my
mental
health

and i just let it
be

what would it be without them?

or am i the only problem?

we will never know
if i can't finally let them go

everything is temporary anyway

i shouldn't care

i wish i understood
love
the thing everyone talks about
i swear to god,
i tried

i tried so hard

but i just don't feel what you do
all i feel is

emptiness

it's freedom but also
forever being misunderstood

-aromantic heartache

it's just a
wishing
more like a
yearning
internal screaming
that you are not hers
that you are not mine
that nobody is anyone's
because you all are living a life
i don't understand
and i feel

foreign and left behind

-i don't even wanna be yours

the smallest
inconveniences
are like

bulletproof
shot into my stomach
suicidal idealization
wanting
harm
kill
destroy

myself
everyone
the world

i wanna leave

it's sensual and sexual
heartbreak
i don't want your future
i wanna be your
best friend
fantasizing about
touching you

anywhere

but it will never be you
and also not her

because since people started
dating

casual touch became
weird for
them

yes, i found
something

that makes me light up
no matter how badly

my whole mind
surroundings
circumstances

might be

it's called mbti

i don't remember how it started or i got
into it

but i'm not likely to ger
out

-i feel the same about pole

if there is one thing i
learned

the aro community holds
so much
love and acceptance
inside

more than most others

and this ain't a
paraoxon

i will forever wonder whether i
crushed on people
romantically
or if i was just
obsessed

they have only been crushes
when i thought
i wanted romance

i thought romance would save
me from
myself

amatonormativity truly
kills

find yourself
someone

who enjoys the same sport as
you do

or similar
who will take you outside

to train
and teach

you worlds, unknown but kind of
familiar

the lockdown knocked us out but

aerialists stick together

this song, again
like twelve weeks later
alone with someone else in
mind

sitting
alone and suddenly
it reaches your heart
and it finally feels right
but not right
enough

i mean, i felt it
it showered me in endorphines
because finally

finally, finally, finally

i could feel whatever they could

but both times it was equally wrong and
painful

it shouldn't be

the relief that
goes through the body
when you realize there was nothing
wrong
with you
from the beginning

you see them living the norm
but know
you can break out
and no one can force you to participate in it
anymore

polyamorous/aromantic solidarity

-at first i thought i would break out as a joke

how didn't i know
earlier
i only wanted crushes
marriage
engagement
"love"

for their attention

not my partner's
but everyone else's

-an aromantic with hpd

i knew i was aro
when i tried my hardest
to relate to love songs
trying to feel what they
feel

but it never worked

it's not like i didn't try
i spent my youth trying to love people
that i didn't
because i didn't love myself

now i do
admiring my aromantic self

it will be alright
i will be alright
i'm not broken

never been

chapter three

summer

and the third tragedy

whenever someone new appears
and it feels really great
I expect it to last
forever
ever
never
never ever lasts
temporary is forever
and forever stays the same

-3 days before this one tattoo

dissociative amnesia
is more than goddamn
real but
yes, you made it worse
but reckless turning mania
gave me freedom
you made me feel free

until your silence put me into
chains

their marks will not be seen
but be forever
felt

-tragedy nr.3

you made me wanna
bleed
but even though i didn't grow
out of
sickness
my blood isn't yours to shed
be shed for
it's mine

you're not even worth my
tears

-grown out of my own bullshit

what i learned this year is
that
no matter how nice something
seemed to be
the loss or change
will leave me more shattered than
i ever was before
that's why
i'm keeping a distance
not even knowing it 'cause
a hundred dancing butterflies turn
into thousands of ravens
a million hurricanes
or trillions of guns

t-thatshootme-tillib-bleed
bleed you out

i never do
it's just another step closer to almost losing my
life

it's never worth it

-am i healing or just growing cold?

i look through my old
poetry
the twelve books i never
published
that made me heal in disastrous
times

dreams of being sixteen
knowing how young i was
what i never wanted
wondering what staring at this will be
like when i'm

twenty-four

i know how toxic
this is

but i want my friends for
myself

their romantic relationships to
shatter

them clinging to me
always

but my rational side just wants them to be

happy

but it makes me feel restless

eating me alive

because i'm different

-the thing i always think and never should have said

imagine being so
numb
that you forgot you really had
two
suicide attempts

and two planned death days
on other days, too

-i wasn't even fifteen yet

sometimes i wonder if i would still
call you best friend

if we didn't grow up
together

because you don't seem to
understand

we live in different worlds

i love you, right?

but you've grown distant

and we're not who we used to
be

calling her best friend feels so much more

natural

you're my sister

drawn to me by blood

it's weird between us

but you'll always stay in my heart

-something that i could never say to your face

you might have fucked me up
but the way you fucked me
healed parts of my
sexual trauma

we might have been reckless as
hell but my ocd got
better

you threw my routine away
and for once,
it was worth it
-sounding ixtj-ish

it's not the desire
for you to fuck someone else
it's not the romantic feelings
arising for her
that bring me to knees

the silent treatment does
the knowing-you-will-leave-me-for-her
does
the betrayal does

knowing my bpd was right this time

does

-tragedy nr.3

she's been some kind of
angel
but it's hard to let go
and commit to
something
while he was still in my head
so disappointed

you made me heal
a little
but sometimes
things are meant for a while
not to stay
present

i made a
friend and you helped me
forget them

a little sister
who reminds me of
myself

-after tragedy nr.3

so many of my tragedies
begin with unhealthy
obsessive
situationships
romance or friendship

things go horribly wrong and
many times
it's my fault without
noticing

and it ends with whole friend groups
unfollowing and hating on
me

tragedy 1 and 3
were differently but
ended the same

-"i'm gonna love you until you hate me"

she might be
more the kind of girl
who fits into your messed up life
who doesn't have her shit together
but is easier
to deal with
BUT

she won't ever be as obsessed with you
as i was

no one will

don't you dare play with bpd bitches

-tragedy nr. 3

my fear of men
let me become scared of
my   .
own
hidden
masculinity

don't hide away
nothing to be afraid of anymore

-coming out, again

you don't know how hard it
is
i'm lithromantic
the feelings i had for you
vanished after our first
hookup

but i made you my
fp
because i didn't wann push
you away

you knew it
you knew my bpd

i know, wanting to propose manic
wasn't right
after like 3 weeks

but still
you knew what i did for you

you made me gaslight myself
and your friends gaslit me

i tore myself apart for you

and you

you left me to die

-i hope your insides get turned out, tragedy nr.3

watching people pass
through late summer air
fading sun but
rising smiles
life's back in the streets
words back in my
mind

breathe in
breathe out
2017 summer feels

but without the endless
pain

i thought recovery
would take those words away

but it just makes them shine
clearer

the days keep running
and running and
running
please don't go so fast

is it the happiness?

please stay don't leave me
every day i'm the
main character

who designed their own
life

but please don't run so
fast

i don't wanna die

please

the more feminine i
feel
the more i'm into
women

the more masculine i
feel
the more i'm into
men

sometimes the switches get so
hard

that the attraction almost is
exclusive

for one gender only

i don't understand

what is it called
when i enjoy kissing
more than
anything,

but

kissing men is gross and disgusting
and i only feel emotionally
attracted

to women

not romantically
emotionally

i need to find out

-not having a more detailed label is driving me insane

the intense desire
of standing somewhere out of nowhere
the thoughts that consume me
"you need to write this. now."

i missed them
they're back

-09/07/2021, 11:52pm, coming back from pole and work

some songs are like
certain moments and
activities

they sound the same
it looks the same
from the outside

don't you touch the inside
it'll reveal the truth
you shouldn't see
you should
but you don't want to

some moments are one in a million
you cannot repeat them
with someone else

and you cannot think of someone else
once a song's been connotated with somebody else

it might have been the most
intense
hateful
passionate
horrible
and exciting experience i've had

but also the one that did turn love
into hate
into indifference

and after everything i've been through, this is something

new and
u n k n o w n

-tragedy nr.3

it's about not fitting in
even though you want to
you want me to
i want to
i found the place to find me
in

but the world just overlooks it

-nonbinary aromantic

my gender is she/her
without being a
woman

my gender is they/them
but female aligned

my gender is nothing but
everything at
once

mostly nothing

with a feminine touch

a high femme soul

that has nothing to do with
womanhood

-demigirl vibes

you remind me of
myself

we're similar

i'm guiding you through the years
that were too hard
for me

and when the night eats you
alive

just know

i've been there
and i am still

but it does get easier

-you healed a part of tragedy nr.3

chapter four

autumn

and a bunch of smaller

tragedies

This is the voice in your head that says
"You do not want this"

body sayin' yes, mind screaming no

This is the ache that says
"You do not want him"

because it's not right and the past should have stayed the past

This is the glimmer of light that you're keeping alive when you tell yourself
"Bet I could fuck him"

because i wanna be desired and left alone at the same time

Why do you need love so badly?

i just need validation

Bet it's because of her daddy

he hurt me more than most others

Bet she was brutal and bratty

my dom doesn't like that

Bet that she'll never be happy

let me fucking prove you wrong

and when i decided to
submit
it was something that
scared me at first
but
with the right
trust
it's okay not to be in charge

it's fucking beautiful even

-l

i just wanna wake up
one day
knowing that the money hell
is over

-i don't ever wanna go back

the silence
of a foreign small town

sometimes
of the most known one

they'd call them peaceful whispers

the growls out of
hell's fires

just the same

imagine regretting
every single person
who ever touched your
skin

somehow
leave me alone

my body says yes
my mind says no

and i say maybe
ignoring my gut feeling

falling into spirals of regrets
and then do it
again

just imagine you
wanna eat
literally starving
losing your mind

but you can't.
disgust.
panic.
b l o c k e d.

you really can't.
move or eat or do anything.
p a r a l y z e d.

shouldn't fall asleep starving
i try not to

but sometimes it's
impossible

poetry lives in the moment
the reality of it
i live with amnesia
and forget
what my poems meant

but what you should know is
i mean every word
always meant them

always will

drinking calories

is easier than eating

them but

water scares me

my body cannot take fluids

anything going in

has to leave either way

getting inside of it

got me trembling

other way around

got me crying

the basics just don't work'
it's like i'm not meant for this

i still fight

i. wanna. be. alive.

-2018 me would be so surprised

i've always been uncomfortable

in romantic relationships

partnerships in

general

serial monogamy

got the best of me

now the thought of only attempting them

is the most unrealistic thing

ever

i'm complete on my own

-a lesson learned in 2021

i don't wanna

lose everyone
to
amatonormativity

in a world full of sensing individuals

it's so hard to be an

intuitive feeler

-enfj, please pick me up i'm scared

i know that
dissociation

can fuck up a lot

can make you lose control

can make anything

to hurt you so you don't

get hurt yourself

but if it

i'm not of sound mind

i'm insane

and it's the reason why you're gone

-tragedy nr.4

it's hard to be someone who feels
so much between those
who got numb over
time over
depression over
life

i over-love
i overthink

i overdo

but you can't take my love away

it will stay even though it won't

return

in the way that i'd crave it

the first party of my
life

and everyone adored me
nobody judged
they wanted me to stick around and
get home safe

loving me and what i do

i hope they still love me
sober

-2018's been differently

everyone liking me
getting along

living my dreams
and studying for them

having my passions
and getting better at them

thirteen-year-old me thought they'd be
dead

nineteen-year-old me responds with a
smile

we're alive

living the life of our dreams
life after school is better

mom was right for once

what i learned before:

not matching love languages
can fuck up
any relationship

but what i learned today:

getting to know each other's
love languages
and understanding them

is alright

you're still loved

and for you it's worth trying
to understand

-t

who even needs
alcohol when
dissociation
is one hell of a ride

enough

-they really thought i was blackout drunk

the thought of
this life

to have an

e n d

is the most horrible thought

that comes to my
mind

-i wanna live forever (and i believe in it)

this weird intense
chemistry

after two years

the intense phone call

the hookup

and how everything went back to normal

-let's never mention it again

and i'm still gonna walk those roads
with or without
you

you tell me i am just a phase but

tell me, who isn't?

i don't wanna be with
anyone but

seeing you happy
with her

still cuts deeper than a knife

-two and a half months later

sometimes
before i go to bed
when i lie down

and turn off the
light i
turn it on again

looking to the pole
looking around my
apartment

not believing which life i

finally created for myself

because it does get better for
sure

-forever grateful

you changed
i changed

we
changed

we made things up

i believe your
apologies

-new beginnings, m

i wish people
knew

that i don't understand
shit

because i try my hardest to
fight through this
cloud

that makes reality
impossible to reach since

april 2018

-dissociation issues

good things happen when
you decided to be
good to
yourself again

-10/15/2021

i stopped controlling my

sexuality

and finally, finally

i can experience the intense things
people keep talking about

and truly enjoy
them
too

do i feel more
feminine again

myself

or is it 'cause

pretending to be a whole

woman

is just so much easier

a coping thing and
i can deal with

it

looking like that will never
bring you someone

because fucking is not about
intelligence

my mommy used to say

well mom

for me, *it matters*

and it's so easy to get a man
they're everywhere

i have all rights to
choose

be unapologetic

yourself

the rest will come with
ease

-talking about girls (and with)

i don't romantically fall for
people

i fall for german linguistics
i fall for moves on the pole
i fall for exotic choreographies
i fall for special kinds of food

i fall for the way i light up
when i explain mbti

to others

and i think this is enough

on the surface,
i have it under my
control.

but deep down,
subconscious

one second
one sentence is

enough

to make me fall apart
and want to die.

-emetophobia

imagine you had only
one
idea for your future

and now it probably won't
work out

was it all for
nothing?

probably not.

it kept me alive for
years

and now it's time

for my new adventure.

-it will be alright

every time
i see you something inside me
happens

even when i was still living

monogamous

two years ago
really

you hurt her so
much but we are so

similar

i don't want you as my
girlfriend

but the way i desire
you
desire
you

DESIRE YOU

where did my control go

-toxic air tastes tasty

this russian infp
with the soft voice
skinny legs
long brown hair
mysterious way of

being

took my heart again for the
night

-i always fall for russians.

(and infps, obviously)

it felt like a movie

this night
my first time ever in a
bar

a gay bar
with my gay friends

the close dancing
the look in your eyes
the way i complimented your
voice and language
and how you said no one ever said
that before

outside
your smoke in your
clothes on your
tongue
the look in your eyes
how i kissed you
how you kissed
me

you me against the wall who
cares switching your hands on my
hips your smile your playful
way

the way you let me

crave

you the way you let me
wonder what will
happen soft
moans
the way i could let myself

go all i want is
you

i wanted you before

i can't stop wanting
you

your mouth your body your
mind

you love my favorite
band

we are the same shade of
fucked up

i kinda love you don't ask me
how and why but
can't forget won't
forget

kisses in the
club
and outside

anywhere everywhere

it felt like a movie and
i wanna hit

replay
and repeat

again and again and again

-is this tragedy nr.5?

the best kiss of my life so
far

i don't think i'll ever

forget

-k

it would have been to
naïve
too unbelievable pretty enough to
believe

that i didn't fuck up

again

in obsession but

i still don't know how not to
do this

but she didn't bother
a lot

just another reason why
i
should
leave
you

-it's too hard for me

you and her,
you're not the same

she's my un-biological
sister

you're my best friend

and you will read this

while she won't

-t, i love you eternally

it's not like i
wanna be sad
it's just so

draining

because somehow it all comes
back

in school like situations

-first real day at uni

nineteen feels lonely

of course, it does

you're letting

go

and everything changes

holding on
hurts more

my dear

-i need to understand

the thing with fps is
you don't care less as the show
you they don't
you just care more
thinking

you might be able to

change them but

stop trying to control the uncontrollable

-something i need to learn

i don't know how much i learned
from
the past but

somehow i see patterns
and even though it hurts

i know when to get help
about an fp
now

-i only get help so we can stay healthy, t

will i ever see
when i get toxic or
not?

because with tragedy one
i didn't see
it

but i knew why

neither with number two

with number three
i had a reason

and four and me
were a toxic cocktail

that i got sick of tasting

you are my angel
and you get me like no one
does

you know that i am trying just wanna be

enough

for you

-t

it's almost november
autumn is still golden
not as dark but
even though it's almost

november

and all of the old symptoms are
back

my body aches

i'm still kinda the happiest i've ever been

people ask me how i've
been

i cannot lie
i always say
"yeah, idk, there's a lot going on lately"

for years now
because it's always true

except for three-day manic breaks
where everything seems
fine

it's not easy

the "feeling good" won't just
appear but i can

...

it's time to find the "try" in "tragedy"

i don't feel like i
lost myself

barely talking
socializing does not
help

hopeless

too sick for existing?

will we ever
know we'll never
know

feeling like a child
age regression without
noticing

take care of me

i can't make it on my

own

submission is not
natural to
me

tragedy nr.2 told me
she's dominant in her real life
but wants to give control
away

to me,
it's differently
giving up on control is the
worst

i need it to
survive but always seem to
lack it

i need it to gain it
back

but if you're soft
and lovely
and still having the energy that makes me
submit

you're rare and i'm glad you show me this
side of me

explains why i felt uncomfortable subbing to
tragedy nr.3

-tragedy nr.1 made me realize somehow

doctors
who can deal with your
panic attacks

who want you to be
fine

instead of telling you to
shut up

when you're going through
hell

are worth their weight in
gold

-wisdom tooth removal 2, 1 was traumatic

they tell me i'm wasting my
time

because i sleep for so
long

my dear
i don't wanna be awake
at mornings

my daily rhythm is
alright

and if i sleep so much
there is less time for me to be
manic or
depressed or
dissociated or
anxious or
paranoid or
you... do you get the point?

it's hard enough to live
already

i feel like my
friends

get tired of taking care of
me

and my parents barely talk
to me

and nobody gives a

damn

i gotta write again

-poems or suicide notes?

i mean i am
falling but
way too happy for

suicide

or sudden death

it's a different story
i love my
life

i lost the burden of
drowning emptiness

not whole
but the suicidal part

i talk myself into being
suicidal
talk myself into
cutting but

when i'm there

it's scary to know how deep in little me
was

because i am way too scared to go
back

-"i ain't there yet, but i'm healing"

sometimes i need a
reminder that
life's worth it

the smell of happy pole place
listening to linguistics at uni
talking to friends or
enjoying nice food
vocal coaching

i hate unbusy
days

they make me forget my
self-worth

and who the real me is

-don't leave me alone with my thoughts

yes,
i love studying
but depression makes me
unable to
focus on the right
things

but when i'm able to
it's wonderful

and i enjoy it more than
the regular student

-being present at uni makes me anxious, but it is so much
better for my mind

my best friend
is my world

called her at half past 5
because the world was
falling apart

but all i learned is

even if i crash

she'll be the one to catch me

i love you, forever, t.

out of money
out of energy
out of social strength

i don't understand

they don't
understand

what if i have no future?..

when i meet

men

my brain keeps screaming
"you're too nice to be fucked"

about them or
"you're disgusting, stay away"

i am aesthetically attracted but

when i fuck them
i don't enjoy touching

them

at all

but certain aspects?

i play pretend
i don't need them

i don't know why i always try

maybe

i am a lesbian indeed

just pretty curious

because reality is different from

imagination

and i will just stick

to the label that fits best

at this certain time

maybe not

i am **not**

never mind

when i found out
i need to get
over this i

shattered

but it's still easy
because life is easier when you

don't care

i'm not even myself anymore

-i don't remember how i wrote this

.

i'll stay obsessed with
you

when i don't see you
i'll be fine

out of sight
out of

mind

-k

a friend of mine
told me

that i have been through
hell

and this year
the best year of my life
yet

i caught myself
and didn't let it out
on anyone

and this
this literally means

i am more stable than i
thought

my phobias
both of being sick and
getting injections

were challenged this
year

so much physical
pain and
injections

making me wanna die but

i am brave and
now i wanna

live

i just don't wanna

suffer

anymore

you're a part of
tragedy nr.2

why do you even talk to
me

and why did my dissociation forget

how much i didn't wanna
meet you at

all

-this one girl from university

the thing about tragedy nr. 4
is that there's not a lot to
say

it's been splitting and obsessing for
four years

it's been fighting and kinda getting closer
for two years

it's been me losing control and saying something
stupid

it's not even splitting anymore

it's me leaving before she leaves me
again

it's not my fault this
time

i wasn't in control

and she knows me like that

but i don't even think about her
anymore

i'm just glad i also don't wear her name
anymore

-tragedy nr.4's not worth my words

sometimes i don't know
what i feel about certain

people

because it's this hatred

and suddenly i don't wanna let them
go

do i actually love them

or do i not?

there is no in between

-bpd is a weird thing

when tragedy nr.1 took
place and he left my
life
and i decided to make him leave
forever

which gave me more control

i changed the password in my
laptop to

"ideservebetter2021"

little did i know
that i truly deserved
better

and i lived happier than ever

the early darkness's better
than rainy, muddy

weather

it's affecting me less
and it's really okay

and that's a big thing
in recovery

i wish
i could think like some poly
people

wanting others to experience you
too

because you're incredible

you truly are
and it's the 24th of november

and i can feel it a bit

but please forgive me when i

can't

you went from
being my favorite
ex

and my so thought *twin flame*

to someone

i can't stand at all

-and we finally let each other go

paralyzed by my envy of the night

when the jealousy eats me alive

i am lost without you here

because i found my entire comfort in you

and outside it looks like rain

the water that fills up my lungs

for the last time, I bleed myself dry tonight

because i'll learn to deal with it

and nothing I could ever write
would help you understand this life

because our minds are not the same
but it might help you understand mine

there's so much beauty when your eyes
lay lost in all the city lights

and i will never fail to see it
you seem as free as they are

but when i take off my
glasses

they look so much more

intense

i think those are your emotions
but you always wear glasses

or try to close your eyes

-14112018

(inspired by city lights by motionless in white)

if i learned one thing
from this year it is that
their lives

are not

my life

we don't have to understand

what makes each other

happy

it's literally my life

and society can shut up about it

they can be happy with
romance

i can be happy alone
with cats and friends

it all could be so
easy

but the thoughts are differently
sometimes

when i
let go
of the two people i used to
love

the most i realized

the people from the past were just holding me

back

-now it's even three.

you know
when your fp does not love you as
much as you love
them

you shatter

but you have bpd
you love more than

anyone

no fp could ever love you

as much

so you

shatter

you shatter every time

i don't want your
sexual touch

as soon as we get closer
i want your

time
hug
hold your hand
maybe fantasize about you but

that's enough

and i'm finally coming to my

senses

i don't want your time
i don't wanna hang out for
hours or cuddle

i'm not your netflix
date neither am i
the one to write about

-aroace thoughts

i'm a hurricane
my love is stronger than
superglue

it comes in waves
you might drown in it

i'm not cold
i have the warmest heart you could ever

imagine

it leaves your hair messy and your
chest might remember my hug for

days

i hold the power to break you,
romantically

but i'm platonically vulnerable

how does monogamy work
i hold so much love inside

it's too much for

one

my love's a different kinda special
but i had no idea i'd get it
back

-i,l

we never mention her
name

but we casually talk about
her

right now from
time to time

-dad, i know you love her

i
hate
how the years tore us
apart

because you've been my
life and that's the only reason why i wanna be

fourteen

again

wish i could take your
pain

wish i could stop the
thoughts

wish i could ease your inner world somehow

but i'm only human
a person who's been through the
same

knowing my words won't get through walls

'cause i can't break them for

You

some people have this
aura

around them
this magical kind of
spell

i felt it three times
before

it's addictive

and everyone understands but the person themselves

-c,k,t

she's been all through hell but
don't want you to
know it

she's so full of love but she never could

show it

-and still i can't take my thoughts off you

they say they mean
it but they
don't

and i'm the foreigner again
a phase

just wanting to be something

and as i am protecting the
candle
from the wind
that i interpret to be
your voice

i still try to save you from
yourself

when i said i'll be there forever

i meant it

-30.11.2021, 5 years later

i told you to
let me be there for
you

and light the candle

you listened to me

and it was quiet

this time you didn't take away the
flame

because i am still burning for
you

i wear you on my body

and i can feel you
close

after all these years without you

-30.11.2016

find yourself a best friend
who tries to speak your
love language

on the days you need it the
most

-t, you're my world and even more, the best to ever happen
to me

this has been the first
year
that didn't give me

hell

it gave me a warm feeling while

remembering it

-spotify wrapped made me so happy

our song is my top song on
spotify
this year

followed by the song of
tragedy nr.3

my fp symptoms have been
real this
year but

one tore me apart

the other found me broken
helped me fixed myself
and always stayed

and always will

-ten more songs of this playlist are about you

i found forever
in your
voice

i found it in the way you
describe my new
medication to
me

because i hear weird voices

i found it in your sleepy
voice at 5am

that saved me from myself

i found it in
your stupid jokes
that meet my humor

i found it anywhere

anywhere you are

nobody should ever claim all aromantics can't
love because

the way i love you is more loyal
than i can picture alloromantic
love

romance decays
bpd love, it stays

just like i will

i tried to take my
emotions

and send my love to
several
people

instead of only focusing on my
fp

but as my favorite polyamorous
life coach says

love is infinite

i can't split it
up

it multiplies

and when i breathe out
cold air that becomes
visible

it's just me

letting go of

you

and you can decide who i mean with
that

giving up on a fp
is like
cutting your lungs out
because you lack the air to
breathe
is like
ripping your heart out
because they're all you've
ever felt
is like
your hands keep shaking
you're crying bloody tears
as you sit in the shower
clothed at 4am
because the feelings are stronger than the
meds

it's like you're comatose
and try to kill yourself
by letting go
but in reality, you're drowning

 and it's the only possibility

to save your life

i will never give up on you, t

but i need to give up on seeing you as
my only source of
happiness

"fuck the world 'cause it's my life
i'm gonna take it back
and never, for a second,

blame yourself"

-when i decided to leave my codependency in 2021

december 2021

and as i walked this
way
that made me so emotional
last year at this time
with the music that i connect with
it
when i was feeling like hell
because i didn't see
hope
for the next year

stuck in a relationship
scared of how i'll
feel
right now i feel
lighter

as if it never hurt
or had an emotional
connection

i am healing
healed from this

i've grown so much this
year

and i'm ready for the next
chapter

i danced and sang
in front of
so many people

who have been cheering for
me

and only me at the end

this is where i belong

on the pole
to the mic
to the people

instead of holding someone's hand saying

i love you

that's not what love is
for me

love is being myself
and fulfilling my own

dreams

and when you say you love me
life feels a little more
worth it

-t

bpd is wild

you'll be happily sobbing on december 24
because you're in recovery
everything feels easier
best year of my life
it can only get
better

you'll cry when you get home
anxiety taking your sleep
an overwhelmed hopeless mess on december 25
almost attempting in the
shower

giving up

but it's been the best year

so note to self: please keep going

twenty-five-year-old you'd be so
proud

i thought we'd be
friends for life like you
said

but we were a platonic lockdown
romance

nice while it lasted

for six months

will be forever one of my favorites

it's not completely gone

but it will never be the
same

i'm having a hard time accepting it

-uni friends, chapter 1

and as we laughed
on new years' eve
2021

finally with her instead of
with tragedy nr.1

after 2 years

it felt like we had our connection
from 2015

back

or never lost it

i love you, s
can't wait for our next
adventure

-the end of 2021

Danksagung

danke an jede einzelne person, die hier erwähnt wurde,
auch diejenigen, die mein leben verlassen haben. wir haben
jetzt 2022 und ich bin froh darüber, dass ich mit den
tragedies und vielen menschen abschließen konnte und sie
in diesem jahr gelassen habe. 2021 haben sich viele dinge
entwickelt, ich habe viel realisiert und bin mit mir ins
reine gekommen. ich hab euch ein bisschen durch meine
coming outs und realisierungen mitgenommen und meine
gedankengänge offen gelegt.

niemals hätte ich erwartet, dass dieses jahr so wunderschön
werden würde, als ich meine hoffnung damals in 2020
gesetzt habe, aber 2022 kann nur viel viel besser werden.

ich arbeite noch immer an meiner selbstakzeptanz, aber die
selbstfindung fühlt sich gerade sehr erfolgreich und fast in
den groben zügen abgeschlossen an. alles wegen 2021!

danke, dass ihr mich begleitet habt.
auf eine spannende weitere reise!

viel platonische liebe an euch,

eure/euer dianne <3

danke an teresa, die mir mit dem formatieren geholfen hat und generell unendlich wichtig für mich ist.

danke an isa und lexie, die mir liebe zeigen können wie niemand sonst.

danke an marlene für die perfekte unterstützung.

danke an lea, wegen der dieses buch entstanden ist.

dankeschön.

© 2021, Dianne Foit
Herstellung und Verlag: BoD – Books on
Demand, Norderstedt
ISBN: 9783754345436